Own Your G.L.O.W!!!

It Looks So Good On You!

Shalonda "Treasure" Williams

TruTreasure Publications

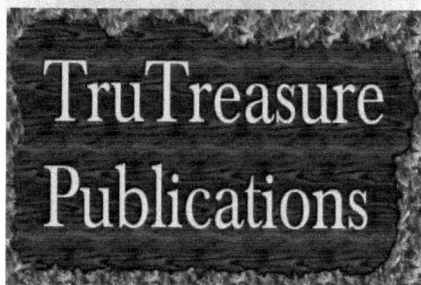

Copyright © 2021-
"Own Your Glow!: It Looks So Good On You!"

Written by Shalonda "Treasure" Williams
Published by TruTreasure Publications along with Kingdom Come
Ministry Productions
Binding and Printing: KDP
ISBN: 978-0-578-90859-5

Table Of Contents

Foreword

Glow a *verb* meaning, to give out steady light without flame.

Glow, also a *noun*, meaning a steady radiance of light or heat. From these two definitions what stands out to me the most are the words light and heat, which when coupled equal *radiance*. As one who loves words, just words in general, there are certain words that get me excited - especially words that speak of light. Prophet Shalonda Williams is coming through loud and clear with this breakdown of the word - G.L.O.W; **G**od's **L**ove **L**enses, **O**utlook & **W**itness. Whew! The very thought of God having a lens that He uses to filter out the darkness and ONLY see the light of what He created us to be is breathtaking! The outlook for living is radiant when we are able to have an eagle eye vantage point - when we can grab the vision that God has input in each of us, as His children. A song comes to mind when I think of the word witness, I remember as a child singing in the children's choir; *"Will you be a witness - for my Lord, will you be a witness, for my Lord, come on and be a witness, for my Lord, come on and be a witness…"* Back then the idea of being a God ordained, God-chosen, God-loved, vessel to shine for His light, was too much for my young mind to handle, but what I did know for sure back then, that I still know now, is that Jesus is light, the light of the world and I am here in the earth to shine forth His Glory.

As you walk through the pages of this book, I admonish you to seek The Father to make you aware of your G.L.O.W - what is inside of you that brings forth the light, the radiance, and the heat of who God is and has been in your life. Exactly how did you make it over it all and are able to still be standing here, unbroken, unbothered, and unapologetic about your testimony? Not holding back how God did what He did for you. Not being afraid of how your story has made you a unique gift to the whole of humanity and certainly not ashamed of the details of the journey that gave you the shine of God's glory.

I give honor and respect to the women that have chosen to G.L.O.W. here in this book, by having a brief "GlowVersation", as Prophet Shalonda refers to it, and sharing their truths, their battles, and their triumphs. It's not always easy to be transparent with the whole world! You know what I mean? You may revel in sharing your heart with your closest friends and family or even a few hundred people in a room, but the whole world? Hmmm... That requires courage, bravery, and a compassion for others - our light, the way we G.L.O.W. up, often guides others along their journey. So, Daughters of The Most High God and to the author Prophet Shalonda Williams, I honor you for your words of wisdom and truth.

I would be remiss if I didn't share with you my very own acronym of the word so that you know what each of these letters mean to me personally. You ready?

Genuinely dedicated to being myself
Loved by The Creator of ALL
Outrageously and overwhelmingly spirit-filled
Wise in the WORD and the WORLD

Listen, I am living my G.L.OW. out loud! I pray that you are too, and if not, well then, I would say that you have the right words of valor in your hands right now. So, get ready to G.L.O.W. up my dear sister or brother, it's your time to know that you are designed to give off the radiance of your God-given G.L.OW., you are a flame of purpose and you house the heat of the Holy Spirit, so your G.L.OW. is not an option, it is a mandate! G.L.O.W. forth!

Apostle Dr. Marilyn E Porter
Founder and Overseer
The Pink Pulpit© International Convention of Women in Ministry
www.thepinkpulpit.org

Introduction to the Glow

The first thing I think about when I hear the word glow is a light coming from a super dark place. I see a dark hole in the ground and all around me is darkness. Amid that darkness something begins to shine, almost like a light flashing slightly from under the ground somewhere. In a movie, it would be the thing that makes the curious individual walk slowly toward it so that they can explore what lies there. It makes me giggle a bit when I think about those people. They are actors and actresses that are being paid, or not, to be curious and go searching out the thing that is giving off light in a pitch, black area, in the middle of nowhere. What makes them so drawn to it, we wonder? Well, light in a dark place is attractive. It speaks, "Come explore me". I know that this may seem a strange thing to see when I think of the word glow, but it's my truth.

Now, on another page of my truth book, when I think of a God-given glow, what I see are angels or a dove giving off some gorgeous light that can be seen for hundreds of miles by people in different locations. All these individuals, standing in places that are nowhere near each of the others, experiencing the same radiating, beautiful and awe-striking view. It is one of the most beautiful visions to have. And they were shining in such a way that nothing dark could even been seen. This glow is one that can not be mimicked by anyone. I know that TV and even some drawings can give a pretty good idea of how magnificent it is, but the reality is that it is God-given, so it is too amazing to copy in any way. This glow also draws many. It will cause us all to stop in our tracks and just gaze at it, unbelieving. I mean… Amazing, right?

For a long time, I did not associate myself with such a beautiful thing. Not either perspective. I didn't feel attractive or as if I drew any attention. It was like I was a part of the darkness that I spoke of above. I was very loved by my family but, in my mind, that was supposed to be the case. I didn't realize that people would or could be so cruel. I thought everyone was as loving as the family I had, but I was in for a very crazy awakening. If I did have a glow, which I believe I did at some point growing up, it was most definitely dimmed by life's challenges and circumstances. I was thrown into a state of shock at a very young age. Bullies were real and so were people who didn't want others to be too nice or be so happy. I had to learn, eventually, that there is always a root to how individuals get this way, but at that time I totally didn't get it and it hurt me badly. Come to think about it, the very thing that I just shared is a root cause.

It was because of how others treated me and the things they said about me that caused my dimming. We respond to what we live through and with. I was tired of being bullied and treated like an outcast so I, too, became a little rough around the edges. I began to get a seriously awful attitude with others, and I tried my best to build a wall to protect myself. It didn't work very well because at my core I still had the same heart. I even attempted to be a bully a couple of times. One of those times resulted in a girl, that I was supposed to be friends with, getting so angry with me for following her around and taunting her that she pinned me up against a wall. Whewww! I watched her face as she screamed, "Leave me alonnnnneeee!!" and all I saw was fear, frustration, and her disappointment in me. She was hurt that I was participating. I apologized to her and explained what happened and why I did it. I wanted her to know that I was wrong for trying to be something I wasn't, just to fit in. I wanted her to know that I was crying out from some place deep too but couldn't explain where. I wanted her to know that I didn't really want to hurt her, but that I didn't know what else to do. Yet, it wasn't for her to understand my silent cry. None of it changed the fact that what was once the glow of a loving little girl was now a dim flicker about to go out.

See, I am aware that there are things that can cause any of us to lose our glow, but if I can help it, I'm going to help as many as possible to find it again and own it!!! It's your glow and nothing should have that much power to dim it.

The word GLOW, now, has a new meaning for me. It is more personal. The truth is that, in order for me to really appreciate this definition, I had to be in that darkness I spoke of. I had to also be that little girl who was provoked into a place that she was not comfortable. I had come to think of myself as just another person that needed to give off this little flicker of light from my pit for anyone to be drawn to me. This is what I thought. These thoughts led me to a darker place. But God is so gracious and loving that He chased me down to make me see things and myself from a different set of lenses. In another book of mine, entitled *Nawww... I'm Not Ok!: Excuse Me While I Unmask*, the ninth entry addresses God as the "God of the Ungloved Hands". In this chapter of the book, I speak of how I came to be known as Treasure. I tell the story of how the name was given and why it was so relevant. One of the main things that I needed to emphasize in this chapter was about how God loves me so much that He can handle me, my dirt and my dark places without having any gloves on. People feel like you are too dirty but LORDDDD have mercy, His eyes have a different viewpoint of me. It is because of His view of me that I can own my glow now and not let anyone or any circumstance dim it. It is mine!!!

My new definition for the word GLOW is this: I am now seeing myself through *God's Love Lenses... His Outlook and His Witness*. My My Myyy what a beautiful sight!!

You ever hear someone tell a person that is in-love or pregnant that they have a glow about them. What they mean is that there is something shining on or in you that is showing up on your face and it is glorious. Well, that's what I know to be true about my glow. People can see it and it feels amazing because it means that I am resting very well in the fact that my

God loves Him some me and He never ceasing to remind me of that love. I got that GLOW yall and I am owning it! Join me why don't you.

Oh yeahhhh… Let me tell you that there are some others that have accepted theirs too and throughout this book and at the end you will get a chance to be encouraged by a few words from them.

So, let's go! Let's own our GLOW together.

I love you #justbecauseican,

Shalonda "Treasure" Williams

Chapter 1 –
Born with a Glow

Before I ever knew what a glow was, I guess I had it. My family was always reminding me of how beautiful I was or how special I was. Over time I begin to see things about myself that made me feel pretty and smart. I knew what it felt like to be cutesie with pigtails and everyone complimenting my mom and me because my hair was thick and long. I definitely knew that I was special to those in my world. All of my siblings were older than me. I am the baby on both my mother's and father's side. My brother, Sam, is the youngest next to me from my mom and he is 11 years older. My brother, Pookie, was the youngest to me from my father, until I later found out about Tammie. They were 7 and 8 years older. So, nope, there was no one close to my age, so everybody played 2nd and 3rd mamas and daddies. I was pretty spoiled at that time, I think. So, it was only right that I thought that I had some sort of glow. Well, they acted like I did. Lol.

Seriously, reaching for the stars didn't seem so impossible back then. My family was great, and they really made me feel loved and sheltered. I was happy when I was that young and I smiled a lot. I was a giver even then, so I found joy in making friends with kids and adults alike and giving away things that I thought they needed. I could talk to anybody and make good conversation. I sang in the youth choir and was pretty good at playing pretend games. I think I was a pretty good actress. (Still waiting on that ultimate role). But I thought I good at a few things and I was smart too. I saw what I felt in others and I wanted to be like those others who seemed to have some sort of glow too. I saw in celebrities and in the singers at church. I saw it big time in certain actors and, also, in some of those powerhouse preachers and most definitely the people who came in town and told people what was going to happen in their future. I saw it in a few of my teachers, too. When I think about it now, I think I was just to that thing inside of them that resembled me.

I recognized something shining and I never really understood why some people were so dark. I didn't know that dark was the word for it until later in life but now I know. There were some who glowed and there were some who didn't. I believed that I was one of the ones who did. There were people who told me something along those lines. But, as I grew, I came to understand that those that I felt were in the dark didn't want to see the people with the light, the glow. I went through some things that proved this to be true indeed.

With all that, I still wanted to be a loving person… still wanted to feel accepted and loved by others too. I mostly wanted to feel it from people that didn't have the same thing I did. Now, I know that this seems backwards, but it made perfect sense to me. I wanted to be like and connected in a deeper way with those who had what I saw in myself yet, I wanted to love and be accepted by those who didn't. I honestly believe that it was a part of what I know now to be a good quality within me that wanted to give them something to help them have light too. They needed it actually.

Oh, but a lot happens inside of a girl who sees through flower filled, rose colored glasses. New lessons are learned that can change you forever if you allow it. Maybe that's what happened to some of those who didn't have that glow. It could have very well been that they were born with the glow and they tried to help others out of the dark and were overtaken by it themselves. What happens when all you thought was true about the world and people turns into a perceived lie right before your face? How do you explain what you see and feel to others that are not and do not see like you?

Chapter 2 –
De- Glowed

The prefix de- is a very interesting thing. It gives a whole new meaning to a given root word. It changes it from something that is there to something that is not. What do you mean? Well, if I have a word such as compress, which speaks of pressing something down or close together; to squeeze something together, or putting pressure on and then you add de- to the front, what do you get? You get the word decompress which means to relieve or reduce the pressing, pressure, or the squeezing. Some of you had much pressure applied so you know good and well how good depression feels. When that relief comes it is so refreshing.

Or, if you take another word like humanize, which is to make a thing more humane, to make it a tad more civilized. It also means to attribute a human character to something. With this word one is adding some more humanness it! And you add de-, what do you get? The word dehumanize is made. This word speaks of when one deprives someone or something of human personality, dignity, qualities, or treatment. It is when lower than human treatment is presented, and it causes someone to feel extremely low. Many of you have also endured this so I know you understand. One minute you were being treated like a whole person and then come de- and changes everything.

Let's do one more. Say you have the word glow, which talks of having a steady light, intense color, or a minor shine, and having a look to your skin that is because of a healthiness or warmth. It is radiance of heat and light that is constant. And it also speaks to a feeling that is strong of well-being and/or pleasure. There is something there that provides a radiance so strong that it sort of oozes through the pores. But when you write a book and decide to bring de- to the party so you can drive your point home, and you add de- to the beautiful word, which I'm sure is probably now a unique, new word, what does it mean? LOL! Yup, you guessed it chile, you get de-glow! This word can only mean that glow has been stripped of the strong feeling of pleasure and well-being. It means that the radiance is gone yall. My goodness, de- did compress a service but it just jacked glow all up.

Well, take that definition and there you have what happened to that little girl. No longer did she feel the radiance that was once there. Here is my truth that I shared with my sister once. I barely remember being happy in life more than I felt sad as an 8 to 30 something year old. I do remember moments where I was happy but what I tap into more as memories are the moments where I felt unaccepted, unsupported, and misunderstood. This from being left out on purpose to being bullied, it takes its toll after a while. Deep down inside I wanted to still be that same girl, but it was hard. Don't get me wrong, at the core of myself I was still loving and wanted to be there for everyone else, even when they brushed me off for others. There was just something compressing it. I felt like danged if I do and danged if I don't. Be loving and desire acceptance and understanding, get hurt. Don't be my authentic self, hurt self. It was a mess.

There are stories that I have told my mother since I've been an adult that really shocked her. I know that she has dealt with life in her own right and had experiences that made her never want her children to have to deal with them, but it baffled her to know how I was treated. Places she took me to be babysit left me feeling lonely because certain individuals in the home left me out. The children played games without me and some of the adults punished me for things I didn't do. Can you say de-glow? There were so many more incidents.

I think that the hardest part about being de-glowed is that no matter how bad you want back what is missing, you can't seem to figure out how to do that, so you do what you think will help. I started having much attitude with certain people and it became a part of me for a time. I thought that if I were mean back that it wouldn't bother me as much. It wasn't true. I was still bothered and got way more sensitive over time. I would go to the bathroom just to cry my eyes out. Then I started making myself available to be touched sexually because that was going to make me accepted for sure, right? Wrong! In my book, Nawww… I'm Not Ok: Excuse Me While I Unmask, I give my many accounts of not being ok with life and myself. A part of that story is about my promiscuity and sexual addiction. I thought that it was the answer until I realize that this doesn't make that good feeling come back. As a matter of fact, it made things even more dim. I remember getting to the point where I was crying after being touched and later crying after having sex.

I spent years upon years trying to climb out of that darkness. In the dark you cannot even see yourself. I felt myself existing, but I was zombie like through much of it. You know that you are there, present in your body, but you cannot see you. Not being able to see can be scary, can't it? All you know to do is just be and pray that someone will come rescue you from it all. To my family it looked like rebellion but now we know that it was my response to my de-glowing.

There was something else I write about in the book that helped me to start peep out into the light once again. Could it be so that someone saw my flicker of light and decided to come see what was there? It wasn't overnight and if I can be honest, I still think that I need a reminder from time to time. I wrote a chapter with a poem entitled, *Yup, You're Still Treasure*. When God called me Treasure, it changed everything and it's what is responsible for the G.L.O.W. I see today.

Chapter 3 –
The return of the Glow

He called me Treasure and He did it in the most unconventional way. I won't go into great detail here but let's just say, it came from a connection that most people would not believe was a healthy relationship. And it came during a time when I was just coming out of one of the worse depressions I've ever had. If you read *Nawww... I'm Not Ok!* then you know the story. God used one of the most unlikely people to remind me of who He created to be before life began for me. The key words that will always stick with me are these: "A treasure is still a treasure even beneath the dirt. It just doesn't know it".

Again, I won't go too deep into the story about the God of the ungloved hands, but I must share briefly in order for you to understand how I got to glowing. I was pen pals and later the lady friend of a prisoner who had been given 25 years in prison. He was the coolest dude, and he was even more country than me being from Atlanta. LOL. We were tippy toe tight, as he would say. We talked a lot about God, and he schooled me on many things that I still appreciate knowing to this day. We wrote every single day and we always had something to say to each other. Once I asked him what name he would call me. Honestly, I don't remember why I asked. I may have been looking for even more validation or I could have been trying to find a new name to be called when I did spoken word. Now, he had a few names for me already, so I don't believe it was about a new pet name. Either way, he said, "I would call you Treasure". I asked him why and he wrote a poem to respond. And those key words I shared with you above were apart of that poem. God used him to tell me that I was still His treasure even while covered in dirt.

See there is something about being loved just as you are. Sometimes it the hardest thing to accept but it is still refreshing to hear. This doesn't mean that the one who loves you doesn't want you to be able to grow into a better and best version of that self. It means that while you do it, they will remain in love with you. My friend was speaking of himself in that message, but He was speaking from the heart God. He told me as much. I understood clearly. I knew that God was sending me a lifeline and he didn't through a man that I have still only seen face to face once since we got acquainted in 2007. He used someone who did not love me for my sex, because we never had it. A person who I told all of my dirt and who could empathize with me because he had his own sins to bear. This was not about him being in prison because he was there for a crime he didn't commit. He just understood that there was a root to much of what I had done and how I lost my glow. God used him to remind me that He knew me deeply and he still thought that I was good and valuable. I was profound. God found a way to restore my glow. There is something major about being loved completely. It changes things within you, and they display themselves outwardly.

I remember when I started dating my, now, fiancé, Marco. At first, I didn't announce it because I was so used to things failing for me that I wasn't sure that I wanted anyone to know until later later later on. Keeping it hidden didn't work. I couldn't keep it a secret. I started smiling more and I was super excited about regular, everyday life things. People started saying things like, "Wow Prophetess, there is something different about you.". So, finally, I announced it on one of my We Flow Virtual Ministry Encounters. "Hey everybody, I want to introduce yall to someone." There were a few on that night that already knew so there were like a kettle ready to explode when I got it out. It was hilarious!

As soon as I introduced to some and presented to other my love, I started getting messages from people saying, "I knew it was something Prophet because you have been glowing". I would smile and say, "What do yall mean I'm glowing"? I just knew I was happy and at peace. Marco and I have known each other for 30 years and he's always liked me, even when I was mean. We were friends and would check on each other from time to time. This time I reached out and he was the same as always. He wanted me to know that no time of day or night was too early or late for me to reach. And this time God said, "Let him love you" and I did. I had excitement because the hope that I had for love was being fulfilled but, I didn't call it a glow. But I believe there was a reason for that. I could not see what was happening because I was the one exuding the radiance...

I am in a relationship that brought out in me something that attracted others and made them hope again. Well, now, I want you to take that story and see something. Marco is a part of what God has given me because He loves me most. My children, family, and friends He gave me because He loves me best. A worthy purpose and call to live out He gave me because I'm His Treasure and He has always meant for me to shine out loud and not be hidden. Wowwww! What a feeling I'm feeling right now just recounting these truths. And that, my beautiful people, is what causes this even more radiant beam I'm displaying. One day when I woke up, I went in my bathroom as usual but when I looked in my mirror, I saw it. What did you see Shalonda? I saw the G.L.O.W. of course!

Chapter 4 – God's

I know this seems a strange title for a chapter. "God's what?", you may be asking... well, nothing right now. I just want to address the 's on the back end of the word God. The 's represents something, and it is a big deal in this regard because it is what's going to make the rest of the chapters make sense. It means that possession is established. And in the chapters to come I am going to show you what God has possession of that has caused me to look at life and myself from a different vantage point.

When I think of what I once thought that He thought of me, I give blank stare. I go far away in my mind's eye and I see the girl who thought that light was in between my legs. But now my mind's eye has been redirected to a new sight. It is the sight of someone else watching me. I get a front seat to the show and that is majorly awesome and scary all at the same time. It's the greatest artwork very rarely realized. The picture of God looking at me through His love lenses, His outlook & His very own witness.

To be continued…

Chapter 5 –
God's _Love _Lenses

When I was studying the word lenses it captured my attention for a long while. At some point I thought lenses only to be about glasses that assists many people to see more clearly. I have heard statements such as, "You are seeing them through rose colored lenses or glasses" or "You need to change your lenses because those you got on, are smudged." But, here again, both make me think of something that is outside of your eyes that is helping your vision. One speaks to lenses helping you to see things from a happy go lucky or a silver lining type view. The other is saying that the lenses that you are looking though are not allowing you to see him, her, or life clearly. The only definitions I saw at first only spoke about glass or some other transparent piece of glass or water that helps concentrate and disperse light rays.

However, as I searched to get a better understand I came across something on Wikipedia that mentioned the eyes having lenses. Not glasses but it's very own lenses. Now that changed something in me. I was ready to talk about God seeing us through His assisting frames but just like that He gave me a whole new view. These lenses do assist but they assist what it already built in you for you to process light. Your

32

lenses are transparent and flexible, and they assist the cornea with focusing that light that you see. What is so special about them is that were created to have a very short focal length. This means that it is how we see things nearby or should I say, up close and personal. The lenses are flexible so that it can stretch itself as needed for that up close view. Over time it can lose flexibility making it hard to see things near you. This is very profound because what's the nearest thing to us? Isn't it us? My my my! Over time our lenses may start to cause us not to be able to see us clearly.

Now, just as we have lenses that are naturally ours so does Our God. So, guess what? He doesn't need any assistance to see you clearly. His lenses are 20/20 all day every day even when you find yourself beneath the dirt. Why? Because His lenses cause light to hit you from every angle and love is the driver. Love being the key factor with Him and it being unconditional means that the lens He has never stretches out to the point where He can't see you. It makes me smile when I think of all of this because the lenses being a near distance thing implies, in this case, that He has to be right up on me to see me. It speaks to my point that He will see my dirt and still love me.

If you know anything about love, then you know why this is so important for you to grasp. Love gets up close and personal and it can see everything about you and still want you. His love lenses are all that and I am forever grateful for that. The word love in the sense that I am using it is from the word agape. This word is a Greek word that speaks of love, goodwill, esteem, and benevolence. It is also a word that deal with preference. This love that God is bestowing on you and me every day is His preference, His choice.

Consider lenses that are filled with unconditional sight of your goodness even when all you see is darkness and dirt. Picture these lenses looking at you very closely and seeing your scars, stab wounds, bitter heart, and your tainted thoughts. Now just take it all in that these same lenses sees you as a beautiful, good creation worth choosing to love despite it all. After you think about all of that I want you to put this book down for 30 seconds and begin to give praise and show Him love right back. Tell Him thank you right now and even embrace yourself and imagine that those are His arms. His lenses are shatter proof, do you hear me? His vision is so perfect that He sees perfectly even in the darkest of places. My God! How moving to know that this is your every day, every hour, every moment truth?

Chapter 6 –
God's Outlook

The word outlook means this: A person's point of view from a particular place. A mental attitude toward a thing or a view. The term point of view speaks of a certain attitude or a particular way of seeing or considering a thing. It about the position is which something is observed or look upon. These definitions alone help us to understand a couple of things. For instance, in scripture it says that "All things work together for good for those who love God and who are thee called according to His purpose". There's also one that says, "For I know the thoughts I think toward you". This says a lot about God's outlook concerning His creation, concerning you and me.

His place of viewing is nothing like ours. We begin to look sideways at anything that doesn't look good for that moment. There's no bigger picture. I say all the time that we see things one block at a time. If that is truth, which it is, then God sees the street from its beginning to its end. That's how He sees each and every one of our lives. That's why He knows that, like MC Hammer once said, "Heyyyy… It's All Good"! So, are yall ready for this? Say, "Ahh Huh!!"

I want you to go back a second and think about your outlook on life. Write it down right now… and I want you to be honest with self… Ready, set, go!

Now, I want you to think about your outlook of self and do the same thing… You ready? Get set! Go!

Now, I want you to collect 5 scriptures or affirming quotes about how God feels about you and I want you to write them down… All 5… Go!

Now, just hold on to those for a bit… let's talk about God's witness…

Chapter 7 – God's Witness

You already know what we are about to do here. First things first, let's define the word witness. The word means that one has seen an event or situation take place. It is to have knowledge of something based on your own observation of it or your very own experience with it. It tells of giving evidence of or to testify of. Would you say from these definitions that God is the one that has witnessed more concerning you than anyone else you've ever encountered or built relationship or connection with?

I don't want anyone to get things twisted up in this newly realized state. God still is not happy when we are wicked or evil minded or at heart. He detests certain things, and we can understand why when we step back and look at where we were and how grimy or rachet it was. Don't get offended now, let's take ownership. However, this book was not written so you can go back to muttering over every detestable thing you've ever done. We know that just like any other parent or even lover that doesn't want to see the worst in us, neither does He. So, yes, God has witnessed some things that made him angry and jealous. Yet, ohhh Yet, there is something endearing about this here love He possesses for us. This outlook through these love lenses has put us in a position for what is called grace and mercy. Those two words are golden oldies and still playing for us daily.

I want you to do some more writing. I want you to think of at least 10 things that someone could say they witnessed about you that wasn't so great. Jot them down quickly. (Sidenote: Don't read past this... do the work). Ok... GO!

Now hold on to that for a second and let's chat a little more about the type of witness we have on our side. There are many through scripture He has given good witness. Job was upright and a God-fearing man. Enoch was a righteous man. Jesus was His Son in whom He was well pleased. Moses was His man for sure. Abraham had it counted unto as righteousness that he had faith. And David, oh David, was a man after God's own heart.

I want you to understand that with all that has ever been witnessed concerning you by others, God has thousands of other good things to say concerning you. God's witness says this: I saw you when you owned up to your part in that situation that caused someone else to be hurt. You didn't lie to get on their good side. You were honest and I am so proud of you. I witnessed when you were going through pain in your body, and you still prayed for someone else pain. That was so selfless. I was there when they lied on you and you still wished them well. You didn't even hold a grudge. That takes a lot of pureness in one's heart and you did it. I spoke up for you when people wanted to throw you away because you kept getting pregnant out of wedlock. I saw your push when you had to work two jobs and finish school at the same time. I cheered for you when you were running and running without anyone else there to support you. I was there when you turned down the temptation and took the way of escape I provided. I saw you! I see you and I am so very proud of you.

It is a sure thing that we have the greatest witness there is. It is because He sees you from His love lenses from the greatest outlook ever. Now there is only one thing left for you to do because you know these truths... It's time that you ... (Turn the page please)...

Chapter 8 –
Own your G.L.O.W.

That's right! I'm dramatic and I had to make you turn the page to tell you that it's time for you to own your G.L.O.W.! It is time for you to start seeing yourself from God's Love Lenses, Outlook & Witness. It's a beautiful thing to behold. But this part is going to take some work on your part. Yesssss!! (I wish I had that little baby GIF to put in here. I love that kid).

One of my favorite scriptures in the bible is Romans 12:2 In the Amplified version. It says this: "And do not be conformed to this world [any longer with its superficial values and customs], but be transformed *and* progressively changed [as you mature spiritually] by the renewing of your mind [focusing on godly values and ethical attitudes], so that you may prove [for yourselves] what the will of God is, that which is good and acceptable and perfect [in His plan and purpose for you]".

The one part that sticks out to me the most, as we read about being transformed by the renewing of our minds, is the part that says progressively changed. That word means, in a steady and innovative manner. A way there is forward and onward looking and the motion is in stages. It's very important to understand it. I had to myself. If I didn't, I would still be in the dark dirt unsure of who I truly was to God. It took time and it took steps that led me upward and out.

It is my desire that you would fully embrace this owning! Owning your G.L.O.W. is the whole point of this work. The word own speaks of possession and belonging. I need you to possess in such a deep place within. It would suck to sit here and read this entire book just to put it down and still feel the same about yourself. It's time to let God love you so completely and well. It's time for you to come to the full understanding that He loves you so limitlessly. When you get this truth and bind it to your heart you will feel it and others will see your glow. There will be a new bounce in your stride. Try it and see if what I tell you is true.

This is what I have done and what I desire for you. I have provided a journal section for those of you holding the paperback copy of this book. Those of you reading on your tablet, computer, or phone, I want you to grab you a journal and get ready for this simple task. Below I am going to pose some questions and give you some brief assignments. I want you to promise yourself that you will do them all.

#1 – Consider what you wrote in chapter 6 concerning your outlook on life. I want you to write down, in your journal space, a new response to that question. I want you to take that outlook and switch viewpoints. Take a moment to write down a positive response that you can look at every day, in faith. What a Being thinks is their reality. Because God's outlook on you and what He desires for you is so amazing, I need you to write down an amazing outlook of your life.

#2 – Consider the next question concerning the outlook of yourself and do the same thing. Now that you are embracing the loving compliments of your God, what would you say differently concerning yourself.

#3 – Consider the things that you wrote down in Chapter 7 concerning what others have witnessed about you that wasn't so positive. Now, I want you to think of 30, yuppp, I said 30 things that God witnessed concerning you that were positives. Your wins, your triumphs, your resisting of the adversary, and your big proud moments mean something. You have more than 30 so I'm being nice. But I will say what I always say, there are two side to the number line. The interesting thing is that, for some reason, no matter how many positive numbers are on the right, most of us still look to the left to see how many negative numbers there are. It's the truth most days, for many of you, but NOT TODAY!!!

#4 – With all the things you have written this is how you Own Your G.L.O.W. The word own means to have possession of, right? Well, I need you take full possession of what you have written here today. That requires that you shut out all other voices that will tell you that this is fluff and only a gimmick. I'm no gimmick, nor do I have any for you. The way I climbed out of the place of darkness and dark thoughts concerning myself was by taking one step at a time and reminding myself often that His plans for me were full of hope and prosperity. I reminded myself that I was always and will forever be His Treausre and my dirt was not stopping that. I reminded myself that He called me good from the very beginning. You must do the same. And I want you to start with your own truth and Own that G.L.O.W. I want you to take the scriptures or quotes that you wrote in Chapter 6 and rewrite them in your journal adding affirmative statement(s): I believe that... I know that... I am... etc. Decide today that you are going to reread what you have written every day until you are fully persuaded and in full ownership. Then, let no one or nothing ever de-glow you again.

These assignments will work for you if you work them. I see my glow now and it is too strikingly beautiful for me to let it go. I'd miss it too much. So, for now, I'm going to say "See you later" right here. Don't forget to do the work. Before I let you go and before you dive into your work, I want to share something with you. You saw in our foreword and in our introduction that there would be some GlowVersations for you to tap into. These are short interviews with a few of my friends that I wanted to share with you. They answer some questions for me that I pray will be an inspiration to you. Most of us have lost our glow at some point or another but we are here to own it once again. So did these ladies. #BeNspired

We Glowing!
GlowVersations
With Friends!

We Glowing! GlowVersation with

Tiesha N. Bryant

When you think of the word "glow" what do you think of first? Paint me a picture...

"Singing: Just let your soullll glow! LOL!

LOL! Just let it shine throughhhh!

Yes! But I kid I kid. I think of a pregnant woman. As her stomach grows, the greater the glow. The radiance she displays that comes from within. The unique brightness that shines and overtakes her. It's the look of a new life being created."

Now, when you think of a God-given GLOW, what is the first thing that comes to mind?

I think of pure joy, peace, love, and happiness that shines from within. It's like a special form of air has been blown into the body by God himself. It's overflows to the outer level, hence the glow that people recognize.

What did life look like for you before your glow presented itself?

Life before my glow was a life of uncertainty. I was trying too hard not to be who God wanted me to be. I experienced a glimpse of the glow and decided I want that glow forever. Therefore, I had to submit to God fully and trust Him whole heartedly. I'm not perfect so sometimes I feel that Glow getting a little dim, not because God is taking it away but because I step from under it.

Give me your own acronym for G.L.O.W.

Growing Up...

Leveling Up...

Owning Up...

Wising Up...

The Glow Up is REAL!

Give me an original quote that encourages the reader to own their glow.

"Your glow up won't happen like the next person. It is your glow journey, so embrace it, the good, bad, ugly, and indifferent. The more you grow the brighter you glow." - Tiesha N. Bryant

G.L.O.W. for me means seeing myself from God's Love Lenses, Outlook, and His Witness. Tell me, with this definition in mind, when you came to see yourself from this view and what this meant for your life up to this point. How has it caused you to show up in life?

Seeing myself in the lens God sees me in means everything. I am reminded that I am fearfully and wonderfully made. I don't have to worry about what the next moment is going to bring or how He's going to provide. Why? I am his favorite/greatest creation. I know if He does it for the birds and the flowers, He will, definitely, do it for me. Therefore, I'm able to show up and tell people how good God has been, is being, and will continue to be to me. I don't have to give them a story out of the bible; it's all personal. My relationship is real.

www.tieshanbryant.com

www.wehaveapurposeinc.com

Social Media:

FB: Tiesha Bryant

IG, Twitter, Youtube: TieshaNBryant

Book: *Imperfectly Perfect: Three Steps on the Parenthood Journey*

We Glowing! GlowVersation with
Robin Bella Lewis

When you think of the word "glow" what do you think of first? Paint me a picture...

My first thought of the word glow was God's Love on Woman. Next, I begin to think about the definition of the word as it relates to women. Words like radiant, shine, brightness, warmth, and vividness came to mind. I thought of women in the bible that had a glow from the inside that was obviously showed on the outside as well. Positive prototypes like Ruth, Esther, and Hannah became clear examples. Their stories are still illuminating today.

Now, when you think of a God-given GLOW, what is the first thing that comes to mind?

The first thing that comes to mind is my God-given Glow is radiance that illuminates from me to other people. My God-given GLOW should be able to infiltrate the very soul of those who need it.

What did life look like for you before your glow presented itself?

Life before my glow presented itself to me looked a worldly version of a success strategy that did not included God's guidance or design for my life. It was an endless, self- defeating, pointless pursuit that made higher education and brown nosing the only path to succeed.

Give me your own acronym for G.L.O.W.

G- God's

L- Love

O- On

W-Women

Give me a 2 -3 lined quote that is original that encouraged the reader to own their glow.

Believe in yourself while having faith in your abilities. *Once your faith takes action your potential has no limit*

G.L.O.W. for me means seeing myself from God's Love Lenses, Outlook, and His Witness. Tell me, with this definition in mind, when you came to see yourself from this view and what this meant for your life up to this point. How has it caused you to show up in life?

My senior year of college is when I first saw myself from God's Love Lenses, Outlook and His Witness. I started hearing God's audible voice permeate from the depths of my soul. During my prayer time God began to tell me how He would use my gifts, talents, and other factors for His glory. He said He would give me the desires of my heart while enhancing those called to my arena. He was giving me profound revelation and guidance about my future callings and assignments line upon line, percept upon percept. I had always been a confident person; nevertheless, my confidence grew vastly in Him. I remember walking through the grocery store and my smile would change people's persona. I knew it was God's light, His shine, His luminescence, His GLOW projecting through me. He began to guide me through a personal development plan that included mentors, friends, opportunities, and discernment to conquer plotting schemes. I believed every word God speak to me. When he called me to be Motivational Speaker, I knew it was because people needed motivating through Him. When he called me to be a Life Coach, it was because someone needed guidance in my specialized areas through Him. When He told me that my hands were flames of restoration and revitalization, I knew there were people that needed healing and deliverance. When I started to align with God's plan and will for my life, I began to see and feel my GLOW!

www.robinbellalewis.com

FB: Robin Bella Lewis

IG: Robin Bella Lewis

We Glowing! GlowVersation with
Sarah Grace

When you think of the word "glow" what do you think of first? Paint me a picture...

When I think of the word "glow" I think of someone or something that radiates beauty and grabs your attention, stands out among a crowd or other things.

Now, when you think of a God-given GLOW, what is the first thing that comes to mind?

When I think of a God-given GLOW, the first thing that comes to mind is the power of God radiating from within a person showing up on their outside.

What did life look like for you before your glow presented itself?

Before, my "glow" presented itself, I would say it was the opposite. I was dark, meaning I didn't have much in the area of vision, direction, or even a feeling of life and vitality and I definitely wasn't radiating with God's power in any way.

Give me your own acronym for G.L.O.W.

God's

Love

Overflowing

(In a) Woman

Give me a 2 -3 lined quote that is original that encouraged the reader to own their glow.

"Every woman 'glows' different, never think you're not 'glowing' because your 'glow' doesn't look like someone else's. Just like the beauty of a rainbow, every hue brings a unique and beautiful part of a bigger picture. When you 'own your glow' you are owning your beautiful contribution to a bigger picture where we are all reflecting God's glory." – Sarah Grace

G.L.O.W. for me means seeing myself from God's Love Lenses, Outlook, and His Witness. Tell me, with this definition in mind, when you came to see yourself from this view and what this meant for your life up to this point. How has it caused you to show up in life?

I used to want to hide under a rock, and not really be seen or heard unless I had no other choice. Then I realized that allowing God to show His love and goodness in and through me was a way He could be made known to others. Knowing that, I have to own my glow, it's my responsibility to show up and let him do whatever he wants in and through me because if I don't there may be people who don't know who He is and what he can do with a woman who will invite Him into her life.

www.thegrceffect.com

www.commissionedincorporated.org

Social Media:

FB, IG: thegrceffect

Founder of Commissioned Incorporated

Host of Damascus Roads and Daytime Drama

Books: The Woman With The Issue Of Love

Sarah Grace: A Testimony

Faith For The Hard Things: Trusting God When You Don't
Understand

We Glowing! Glow Versation with
Dr. Erica McCrae

When you think of the word "glow" what do you think of first? Paint me a picture...

When I think of the word glow, I think of shining unapologetically. Many of us dim our light to appease others. Glowing in God's purpose for me is accepting who I am in Christ and not being ashamed of the person he created me to be. It comes naturally because it's not a façade. I am who he says I am.

Now, when you think of a God-given GLOW, what is the first thing that comes to mind?

My God-given GLOW is my purpose here on earth. For me to know that purpose, I must spend time at the feet of Jesus. It's becoming all that he created me to be, which is multi-faceted. I still don't know everything that God has for me, but as I put one foot in front of the other, he leads and guides me. I am content knowing that he has a plan to prosper me and not to harm me. I get joy walking in purpose.

What did life look like for you before your glow presented itself?

I was a hot mess. My attitude was horrible. I wasn't the best wife. My life was just not a happy one, even though I grew up in the church. It wasn't until I started living solely for God and walked in my glow that I experienced true happiness. There is nothing like walking in the will of God. It's so refreshing. I thought to myself, "why didn't I do this years ago?"

Give me your own acronym for G.L.O.W

God's Leadership Over Wants – it reminds me of the group he gave me, "God's Purpose Over Everything," not our will but God's will be done in our lives.

Give me a 2 -3 lined quote that is original that encouraged the reader to own their glow.

"When you are in God's will, the sky isn't even the limit to what you can attain. Walk unapologetic in your purpose Queen!"

G.L.O.W. for me means seeing myself from God's Love Lenses, Outlook, and His Witness. Tell me, with this definition in mind, when you came to see yourself from this view and what this meant for your life up to this point. How has it caused you to show up in life?

I had to understand that God was waiting on me to show up. I wasted so many years "running" from purpose. What I realized was God wanted a real yes from me. Not a yes when I was fed up with life. He wanted me to pour out my heart to him and mean it. When I did, he changed my life. He knew I was ready. He extended his love to me and started using me in a powerful way. He showed me, me through his lens and let me know I am good enough. He revealed his perspective and outlook for my life (well, partially because I'm still walking out this journey). I will forever be a witness of his goodness and mercy. I recently started seminary to further my pursuit of him. For the rest of my life, I will serve my God. I will give him a yes, no matter what the assignment may be.

www.ericamccrae.org

Social Media

FB: Erica McCrae

IG: ladymccrae

Products: God's Purpose Over Everything T-shirt line

We Glowing! Glow Versation with
Ashley Service

When you think of the word "glow" what do you think of first? Paint me a picture! (doesn't have to be spiritual)

A bright light that shines on everything within its reach.

Now, when you think of a God-given GLOW, what is the first thing that comes to mind?

Illumination that can't be dimmed.

What did life look like for you before your glow presented itself?

Before my glow presented itself it was very gloomy. Kind of like dark clouds followed me everywhere I went.

Give me your own acronym for G.L.O.W.

G.enuine L.ove O.vercomes W.eariness

Give me a 2 -3 lined quote that is original that encouraged the reader to own their glow.

I don't know everything, but I do know a God who knows all things.

G.L.O.W. for me means seeing myself from God's Love Lenses, Outlook, and His Witness. Tell me, with this definition in mind, when you came to see yourself from this view and what this meant for your life up to this point. How has it caused you to show up in life?

Sometimes when you're in relationships you try to gain their view of you. Unfortunately for those past relationships, I was unsuccessful, and I hardly heard affirming words. Even the simple expression of I love you which made me undervalue my worth. But what I didn't realize is that God was trying to affirm me through His voice while in His presence. When people speak sometimes their actions don't follow through and their words can bear emptiness, confusion, and unfulfilled promises. I've learned that when people get mad and or upset, emotion can become unstable and irrational, however with God His thoughts for me and Word over me will never change despite what I've done or what I've done toward Him. His love will never change.

www.abbascloset.com

Social Media:

FB: Ashley Necole

Product: Abba's Closet

We Glowing! GlowVersation with
Michelle Rouche

When you think of the word "glow" what do you think of first? Paint me a picture...

Like others when I hear the word glow I immediately think of a light. For me the light is soft and radiating. The light is a softer version but NOT a LESSER version of itself. That glow is sometimes called the "it factor". The God given glow can be carefully harnessed in a human vessel. The glow is undeniable. I've often heard people use the phrase, "there's just something about her" OR " I don't know what it is about you". The "glow" is an attraction that draws people to your light. Janet Jackson sang the lyrics, "like a moth to a flame" -- this phrase is a simple allusion to the attraction that moths have to bright lights. THE glow works both ways, you can be drawn in. Make sure that it's a GLOW UP.

Now, when you think of a God-given GLOW, what is the first thing that comes to mind?

A God given GLOW is the ability to walk into a room and everything and everyone takes note. The realization that heaven and Earth have collided. We are Earth but we house heaven.

What did life look like for you before your glow presented itself?

Honestly, I have always been aware of God's BIGNESS in my life. There have been times when I knew the ABILITY of God, but I was unsettled in his WILLINGNESS. I believed He could do it but would He. Would He do it for me? Like others, I prayed the "lottery prayer" -- Lord if it's your will...If it's in His word IT IS IN FACT His will. I have no reason to doubt that my prayer will be answered based upon His words. NOT mine; His. He said that He is a rewarder, so I expect my reward after I've met the conditions of

His promise/contract. I work with contracts every day. In order for a contract to be valid there must first be a meeting of the minds. Unless AND UNTIL I get in agreement with the Creator, we have no deal.

Give me your own acronym for G.L.O.W.

GIVE LIFE (TO) OTHER WOMEN

Give me a 2 -3 lined quote that is original that encouraged the reader to own their glow.

"If you choke on the investment, you will never be able to digest the ROI" — Michelle Rouche

G.L.O.W. for me means seeing myself from God's Love Lenses, Outlook, and His Witness. Tell me, with this definition in mind, when you came to see yourself from this view and what this meant for your life up to this point. How has it caused you to show up in life?

I love the words and their meanings. I believe every word that God gave us is intentional.

When I hear the word lenses, I think of one thing: VISION. Many people use lenses aka glasses to correct vision. When you visit the optometrist, you take a "VISION" test not a SIGHT test. Vision is the faculty of being able to see. Understand that seeing is not merely a natural function. For example, when you read the words RED DRESS, your mind paints the picture of an image- a red dress. We hear in pictures. Read that again. WE HEAR IN PICTURES. It is accurate to say that what we hear affects what we see. This serves as validation (disclaimer: the scripture needs no validation BUT for purposes of our discussion please indulge me) for the scripture (II Cor 5:7) we walk by faith and not by sight. Stay with me. Faith comes by hearing (II Cor 5:17). We can say that we walk by what we hear. When we speak our words are the pictures/images(proof) that what we heard is REAL. The images that we speak begin to take form and exist in another realm. Just because you can't see it NOW doesn't mean that it doesn't exist. FAITH is the currency of the Kingdom. You can exchange your faith for your stuff. FULL STOP-- that was good. You can't become what you can't behold. What do you see when you look through the lenses? If you don't see the promises you may need to adjust your thoughts because thoughts become the things or the pictures.

I challenge you to adjust your vision. Change your language. Arrest your negative thoughts and walk toward the GLOW.

www.michellerouche.com

Social Media:

IG: MichelleRouche

FB: Michelle Rouche

Twitter: Michelle Rouche

Tik Tok: Michelle Rouche

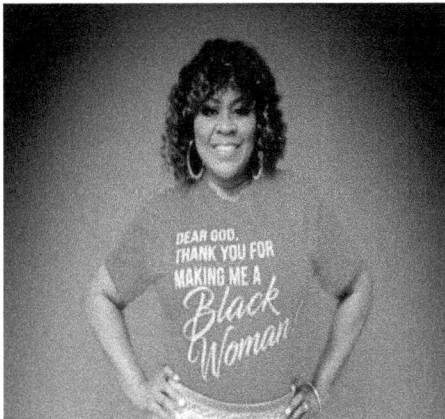

We Glowing! GlowVersation with
Kelli Coffer

When you think of the word "glow" what do you think of first? Paint me a picture...

When I think of the word, glow, I think of something that shines and is set apart. Something radiant and unable to be hidden. The ability to draw something or someone. The ability to shine light in the midst of someone else's darkness as well as your own. I also think of glowsticks and how they shine brightest after being activated through brokenness.

Now, when you think of a God-given GLOW, what is the first thing that comes to mind?

Anointing. I think of it being a like a super-power because it goes beyond us and works despite us. The ability to supersede pass your own limitations and bring healing, deliverance, and breakthrough to whomever you're called to. To mirror the image of God's love and image that will restore hope and life to those in darkness.

What did life look like for you before your glow presented itself?

Life was pretty challenging. The cycles of disappointment and failure forced me into autopilot, and I was focused on daily survival. Everything ran together and to get through the daily was an amazing accomplishment.

Give me your own acronym for G.L.O.W.

Grace to Live while Overcoming your Wilderness!

Give me a 2 -3 lined quote that is original that encouraged the reader to own their glow.

"Silence your inner critic so your outer critics won't matter! You will reach who you're called to. God's love can cover you in your most exposed experiences. His strong arm can reach you in the deepest pits of despair. Ask God to show the big picture through healing will help you trust Him. You're not too broken and you're still fit for the Master's use!" – Kelli Coffer

G.L.O.W. for me means seeing myself from God's Love Lenses, Outlook, and His Witness. Tell me, with this definition in mind, when you came to see yourself from this view and what this meant for your life up to this point. How has it caused you to show up in life?

Life has a way of making you feel like you've been forgotten. When you get hit from multiple angles all at once and days to turn months then years you can become desensitized. Your outlook on life in general is warped and life with Christ can become stagnant. You may feel like God's love may be distant and your brokenness hinders your witness, but it's the complete opposite!

It's because of His love that I'm still here! My mere existence is a constant reminder of who God is! The world will know Him because of my ability to make it through things that would have destroyed someone else! I embody grace, wisdom, victory, and triumph. His love for me is pure and His plan for my life is great!

One more thing too. So many are waiting on you and me! Get ready to testify through your glow!

www.kellicoffer.itworks.com

www.myfes.net/KCoffer

www.ucespp.net/KCoffer
Social Media:
FB: Kelli Coffer
FB: Perfectly Created Ministries
IG: Kelli_03

We Glowing! GlowVersation with
Shayaa Whitley

When you think of the word "glow" what do you think of first? Paint me a picture…

When I think of the word "glow" the first thing that comes to mind is a really bright light with bold color. Yep, a light that pierces unapologetically through darkness. Indescribable and fascinating.

Now, when you think of a God-given GLOW, what is the first thing that comes to mind?

Oh! Now that God-given GLOW…. Now that's what you want!!!! It's that original, that authentic, that unmatched, that self-defining, I can't be bought type of GLOW. This type of glow is an I've been through the fire and made it out untouched type of GLOW. It's that whatever I touch wins type of GLOW, that intrigues others to want to know God for themselves type of Glow. It's a badge of honor from heaven that is tailor made just for you. It speaks volumes even when you are silent. It's that all you have to do is show up type of GLOW!

What did life look like for you before your glow presented itself?

Life before my glow looked like me settling, compromising, not having the strength that I needed to push through hard times, a mouth with no filter, and an ear ready for the next sippin' of the tea. Life was about me being quick to speak and slow to listen. It was a reflection of me being in control and doing what I wanted to do because I could. Life was all about wearing trendy clothes that made heads turn that said "I'm Somebody" because really my character and self-esteem was saying the opposite. Life was me having way too many excuses, me not taking responsibility, and being on fast forward to failure due to running from pain. A HOT MESS!!!

Give me your own acronym for G.L.O.W.

G- Give up on the idea of being your own! (Yes! Put the whole theory in the trash.)

L- Live to understand and permeate true Love. Then maybe you can attract who and what you keep complaining about not having.

O- Open your heart to the ways of Christ and be transformed Foreal! Foreal! God is grading more than your attendance card at church.

W-Work on falling so in love with your relationship with God that you actually fall in love with yourself which is a recipe for finding your purpose and inheriting your GLOW!

Give me a 2 -3 lined quote that is original that encouraged the reader to own their glow.

"Your Glow is YOUR GLOW! You have the right to find and protect your Glow. Those that throw shade on your Glow are probably those who have yet to find their own. Your Glow may hurt their eyes but will be YOUR greatest asset!!!" – Shayaa Whitley

G.L.O.W. for me means seeing myself from God's Love Lenses, Outlook, and His Witness. Tell me, with this definition in mind, when you came to see yourself from this view and what this meant for your life up to this point. How has it caused you to show up in life?

I was in my early 30's when I made a concrete decision to allow God to make me completely over. I had officially had enough of me. I was tired of losing, losing myself, and losing those who mattered most to me. I consistently cultivated a relationship with Christ instead of looking to a man or things to make me whole. I learned to be vulnerable with Christ. There was no room for pride to even have a chance at existing. NOPE! Not this time. I was sold out for Christ. Especially when I noticed He had changed my ways, my heart had healed, and I learned to deal with life's curved balls. What a journey! It was, definitely, far from peaches and cream. When God showed me the strength that I was now operating in, my confidence boosted tremendously, and I don't mean arrogance. My standards changed big time. My desires changed and so did my circle of friends. No love lost. I just developed the mind of Christ which causes you to be more mindful of the way you talk and the places you hang out. My Love for Him has changed my entire life and I absolutely love it. I have inherited my GLOW and I will forever be a witness of the goodness of God. My Glow is what makes my clothes. See, they no longer make me. It helps to transform the lives of others and opens doors connected to everything attached to my destiny! I'm unapologetically Glowing and everything attached to me wins!

www.kingdomsoundradiobroadcast.live

www.facebook.com/wtd101

Host and CEO of What's the Deal

Radio Personality at Kingdom Sound Radio Broadcast of "Millennial Fire"

We Glowing! GlowVersation with
Shetia Jackson

When you think of the word "glow" what do you think of first? Paint me a picture...

To me, glow is the essential light that shines internal, it's as if the sun and all of God's glory is radiating through your skin.

Now, when you think of a God-given GLOW, what is the first thing that comes to mind?

A gift that people get to experience. It's how you interact with people and how the atmosphere changes when you are present.

What did life look like for you before your glow presented itself?

To be honest, I never really thought about it, but I'm a dope individual. I'm coming into my own and owning every unique part of me.

Give me your own acronym for G.L.O.W.

G: God's L: Love O: Overflowing W: Within

Give me a 2 -3 lined quote that is original that encouraged the reader to own their glow.

"Be unapologetically, uniquely you. Learn to shut down and dismiss the enemy's advances and, most of all, trust God and the process even when you are afraid." – Shetia Jackson

G.L.O.W. for me means seeing myself from God's Love Lenses, Outlook, and His Witness. Tell me, with this definition in mind, when you came to see yourself from this view and what this

meant for your life up to this point. How has it caused you to show up in life?

I love this definition of your version of GLOW, I never viewed myself the way God has viewed me until I got older. I knew I was different, but I didn't know that God made me this special. I have a better outlook on my life and how I view individuals and/or certain situations. God's GLOW is causing me to step into uncomfortable situations knowing that I will come out victorious. Getting my fears under control and doing it even when I can't see the end results. I also know that God will take care of his daughters and that he meets me where I am.

Social Media:

FB: Shetia Jackson

We Glowing! GlowVersation with
Jean Cox-Turner, RN, Holistic Health Nurse Coach

When you think of the word "glow" what do you think of first? Paint me a picture...

When I think of the word "glow," I think of true health and the true beauty of a person. Both begin on the inside and radiate to the outer man. I base my practice on nine dimensions of health. When one is healthy from the inside out, there is a glow that flows from within. It is evident in the way they look and in how they feel. That person is healthy, healed, and whole in every dimension of their well-being. This is not to say that one does not have any problems or concerns! It just means that they have made the decision to be resilient, confident, courageous, and their true authentic self!

Now, when you think of a God-given GLOW, what is the first thing that comes to mind?

What come to mind is the Glory of God! The glow that comes when someone is in relationship with God and spends time in His presence. It is a glow that comes from a heart that is pure before Him. An enlightened heart!

What did life look like for you before your glow presented itself?

As a retired Army officer, I allowed the organization and the culture to dictate to me how I should look, how I should act, what to say and how to say it. I also allowed former spiritual leaders to do the same. I have always gone against the "status quo," against the grain so to speak so it was difficult to glow and be my true, authentic self in these atmospheres. If the truth be told, it was not until 2018-2019 when I found myself walking through a "suddenly" health crisis that I told myself that I was no longer going to allow anybody to put me in a box! Those two years afforded me the time to be still, reflect, and re-evaluate. Now that I've totally surrendered to God and am allowing Him to do what He does, I can truly walk in my glow and feel free to be who He created me to be. To go forth in all of my authenticity! Now I'm walking in my glow!

Give me your own acronym for G.L.O.W.

G.L.O.W. - God's girl **L**iving life and **O**vercoming like a **W**arrior!

Give me a 2 -3 lined quote that is original that encouraged the reader to own their glow.

This is a quote that God gave me when I was walking through my "suddenly" health crisis and I included it in my book, "The Spirit of a Warrior!" For this project, I decided to include the word, "Glow".

"Grow & Glow through what you are going through!" – Jean Turner

G.L.O.W. for me means seeing myself from God's Love Lenses, Outlook, and His Witness. Tell me, with this definition in mind, when you came to see yourself from this view and what this meant for your life up to this point. How has it caused you to show up in life?

I came to see myself from this view during 2020 as I was resting and healing from the events of 2018-19. Now, I see myself the way God sees me. I embrace the fact that in His eyes I am fearfully and wonderfully made, personality and all! He created me so He knows the true essence of who I am. I am created in His image. Therefore, I am an extension of Him created to fulfill His will and purpose here on the earth. With that said, I can show up in every dimension, every atmosphere as my true, authentic self and I refuse to allow others to put me back in the box!

www.spiritofawarrior.life

Social Media:

Clubhouse: @nursecoach63

LinkedIIn: https://www.linkedin.com/in/nurse-coach-jean-b4b277159

FB/IG: healthchatwithcoachjean

Twitter: @chat_coach

Books: *The Spirit of a Warrior: Jean's Self-Care Journey Through Chemotherapy*

His Story, Her Story, God's Glory; A Time to Testify

We Glowing! Glow Versation with
Overseer Salena Eason

When you think of the word "glow" what do you think of first? Paint me a picture...

I think of a bright and shining object; something that lights up a room and or person.

Now, when you think of a God-given GLOW, what is the first thing that comes to mind?

I see a person's joy and how they display themselves to the world with unspeakable joy.

What did life look like for you before your glow presented itself?

I was never smiling and always looking serious and in the eyes of others I looked mean. I spent more time working and paying bills not truly knowing how to live and love life.

Give me your own acronym for G.L.O.W.

Guidance

Love

Oil

Wisdom

Give me a 2 -3 lined quote that is original that encouraged the reader to own their glow.

"The CHANGE I want to see must first begin in me. CHANGE REQUIRES CHANGE!!! If you change the way you look at things the things you look at change." – Overseer Salena Eason

G.L.O.W. for me means seeing myself from God's Love Lenses, Outlook, and His Witness. Tell me, with this definition in mind, when you came to see yourself from this view and what this meant for your life up to this point. How has it caused you to show up in life?

I had a glow when I first gave my life to Christ and somewhere down the line life's trials and tribulations allowed me to lose it. I am just regaining my glow and it is a beautiful thing. This LOVE, JOY, and PEACE the Lord has given me are unexplainable. Knowing the agape love, he has for me and how precious, important, and valuable I am to him has made me love myself more. This has also been my motivation to live life and enjoy it with no fears or regrets; but allow the Holy Spirit that lives in me to shine in this dark world. Also living my life as an example of what it means to be Christ Like is my portion. I pray that my glow is so bright and radiant it reaches those that are in the deepest tunnels, the lowest valleys, the smallest cracks, and the darkest caves of their life, and it draws them out to seek God for their G.L.O.W.

https://www.seasonministries.org
https://www.changingseasonsministry.org
https://www.csgministries.org

Products:

www.changing-seasons-ministry.myshopify.com

We Glowing! GlowVersation with
Aquintas Jones

When you think of the word "glow" what do you think of first? Paint me a picture...

When I think of the word "glow" I think of a light shining as bright as an Angel because of God's love and His liberty. Before I received my glow or recognized who I was my light was dim. Now it exhilarates the atmosphere.

Now, when you think of a God-given GLOW, what is the first thing that comes to mind?

When I think of a God-given GLOW the first thing that comes to mind is my Liberty, joy, peace of mind and happiness. Let me break this down: Liberty involves free will as contrasted with determinism. ... Thus, liberty entails the responsible use of freedom under the rule of law without depriving anyone else of their freedom.

What did life look like for you before your glow presented itself?

Life was full of chaos before my Glow presented itself. It was full of disobedience and I did not know or understand who I was and whose I was. I was stressed, depressed, and felt unworthy.

Give me your own acronym for G.L.O.W.

God's

Love & Liberty

Overcame

Wounds

Give me a 2 -3 lined quote that is original that encouraged the reader to own their glow.

"Walk In Your Destiny" - #mylifehasdestiny

"Overcome Your Mask and Walk In Liberty" - #overcomingthemask

"God's Love & Liberty Overcomes Wounds" - #glow – Aquintas Jones

G.L.O.W. for me means seeing myself from **God's Love Lenses, Outlook, and His Witness.** Tell me, with this definition in mind, when you came to see yourself from this view and what this meant for your life up to this point. How has it caused you to show up in life?

When I think of G.L.O.W. (God's Love Lenses, Outlook, and His Witness) I can truly look past my flaws and my circumstances and see me as God sees me. "I Am His Master", He sees me with my light shining as bright as an Angel and I am able to walk in Liberty filled with joy, happiness, peace and peace of mind.

I always said I would not become a byproduct of my environment and I lied to myself and I did just that. I watched my mom in abuse when I was a child. And the cycle of abuse from her trickled down to me. I went through the molestation and inappropriate touch as a child; I also had an abusive marriage and went through spiritual abuse; then married an addict. The cycle didn't break there. It followed my children. But we are breaking the cycle. It stops now. When we broke free this time and walked in our Liberty there was no turning back and no residue of the connections. Abuse is dead in my family, promiscuity is dead, repeated relationships dead. Control & Spiritual Abuse is Dead. I'm walking in my G.L.O.W. My Life Has Destiny and I know it now.

FB: Quint Jones

IG: Mylifehasdestiny,

Twitter: iampurpose,

YouTube: Quint Jones

Books: Get Up & Get Out Your Own Way

OverComing The Mask

Found on Amazon

We Glowing! GlowVersation with
Tijinae' "ParadiseTee" Toussaint

When you think of the word "glow" what do you think of first? Paint me a picture...

Glow: Something or someone who radiates with light and growth. They shine bright and can be recognized by their light, even in a crowd. Never to outshine but to have its own distinguished light.

Now, when you think of a God-given GLOW, what is the first thing that comes to mind?

God-given Glow: As mama and dem say... "Baby, that's the ANOINTING" Psalms 119:105 (NET) His word is a lamp to walk by, and a light to illumine my path.

What did life look like for you before your glow presented itself?

Before discovering my God given glow, I lived in the shadows, opinions, and approval from others. I found Myself extremely self-conscious and doubtful of who I was and my abilities. Others always saw greatness in me, however I struggled to identify that within myself. Once discovering my God-given glow, I had to accept my truth, and that was that God had hidden me. He gave me his heart and I just couldn't go everywhere. He uses me strategically and it's vital I move by his spirit in EACH season. Once I discovered and moved accordingly, I was able to be successful in all aspects of life.

Give me your own acronym for G.L.O.W.

Acronym:

G - Grow and Evolve your thinking first and your life will follow.

L - Light your own path, with self-motivation, and constant reminders that you're worth everything you've ever dreamed of and more.

O - Overly denounce the enemy's tactics, and openly declare your identity and goals!

W - Wait!!! Wait on the Lord!! Wait on your turn!! Wait!! But as you wait... PREPARE!!

Give me a 2 -3 lined quote that is original that encouraged the reader to own their glow.

Quote:

"Leader...Let your GLOW, influence others to Grow!" -Tijinae' Toussaint

G.L.O.W. for me means seeing myself from God's Love Lenses, Outlook, and His Witness. Tell me, with this definition in mind, when you came to see yourself from this view and what this meant for your life up to this point. How has it caused you to show up in life?

Glow from your standpoint:

My favorite scripture is Jeremiah 29:11. It is a direct reflection of the Lord's view for our lives, and it's not always like ours! "For I know the plans I have for you, GOOD and NOT OF EVIL, to give your an expected/prosperous end!! We need to walk in our authority and see ourselves, our spiritual walks, and our lives the way the Lord does and then let that confidence radiate from us!! That's how our Glow can bear witness of his Glory. That's what I do now.

Fb: Paradisetee, Epitome Escape
IG: _paradisetee
Book: "Cries of a God Fearing Sex Addict"
Natural Hair & Skin Line: Epitome Escape
Business: Epitome Business Consulting

We Glowing! Glow Versation with
Bernice Loman, MBA

When you think of the word "glow" what do you think of first? Paint me a picture...

A light that shines in darkness. A light that stands out

Now, when you think of a God-given GLOW, what is the first thing that comes to mind?

The Holy Spirit. A light that shines so bright that it stands out .

What did life look like for you before your glow presented itself?

A mess. I was trying to find my way through life without God's help before. What a disaster?

Give me your own acronym for G.L.O.W.

God's Light Over World's Darkness

Give me a 2 -3 lined quote that is original that encouraged the reader to own their glow.

"Stay obedient to God. Do everything with God's help." – Bernice Loman, MBA

G.L.O.W. for me means seeing myself from God's Love Lenses, Outlook, and His Witness. Tell me, with this definition in mind, when you came to see yourself from this view and what this meant for your life up to this point. How has it caused you to show up in life?

When I finally realized that I am made in God's image, I began to walk in purpose unapologetic.

www.lomancreativeservices.com

www.marketingcampaignhandbook.com

www.lomantraining.net

Social Media:

@lomancs

Book: Marketing Campaign Handbook

Tech training at www.lomantraining.net

Marketing Consultations at www.lomancreativeservices.com

We Glowing! Glow Versation with

Emmanuella Young

Believer, Wife, Mother, Pastor, Mentor, CEO, Recording Artist, Song Writer, Producer, TV Host and Radio Personality

When you think of the word "glow" what do you think of first? Paint me a picture...

When I think of the word GLOW I think of IDENTITY and confidence. I think of an individual who is fearless and not intimidated by others, the greatness they have in themselves and/or is comparing herself to anyone. I think of a young lady that knows her lane because she created it and doesn't need to be compare herself to anyone.

Now, when you think of a God-given GLOW, what is the first thing that comes to mind?

IDENTITY and knowing who I am whose I am.

What did life look like for you before your glow presented itself?

Dark. Because the light was not on. The light of God loves through the acceptance of His Jesus Christ and the light of Jesus shining through me. I allowed darkness of fear to make me dim my light, my glow.

Give me your own acronym for G.L.O.W.

Give me a 2 -3 lined quote that is original that encouraged the reader to own their glow.

"You've been "Called Out To Stand Out" – Emmanuella Young

G.L.O.W. for me means seeing myself from God's Love Lenses, Outlook, and His Witness. Tell me, with this definition in mind, when you came to see yourself from this view and what this meant for your life up to this point. How has it caused you to show up in life?

It meant for me freedom and confidence in who I am in God through Jesus Christ and who He called me to be unapologetic. I sent so many years looking to be validated by man and accepted by man that I dimmed my shine and dumbed myself down to just for in,

www.emmanuellayoung.com

Social Media:

Emmanuella Young (Public Figure Pages)

FB: @eyoungtv

IG: @eyoungtv

CH: @eyoungtv

Ministry Page:

FB: @RescueTBS

IG: @RescueTBS

CH: RescueNY

Business pages:

Stencil Town Inc.

FB: @stenciltowninc

IG: @stenciltowninc

Terrell Knows Inc.

FB: @terrellknows
IG: @terrellknowsnc

Life Path Training & Coaching Solutions
FB: @lifepathtcs
Single: "Sound of Breakthrough"

We Glowing! GlowVersation with
Zakiya M. Knighten

When you think of the word "glow" what do you think of first? Paint me a picture...

When I think of the word glow, I think of how one shines and radiates to the point where you notice a difference in them. It's an external display of what is going on inside of you.

Now, when you think of a God-given GLOW, what is the first thing that comes to mind?

When I think of a God-given GLOW, I think of an abundance of the combination of joy and peace.

What did life look like for you before your glow presented itself?

It was lonely place where I felt trapped inside of me...trapped partially because I knew that, if released no one would fully understand the contradictions of my heart. I was afraid of releasing the pain which I eventually allowed to identify me.

Give me your own acronym for G.L.O.W.

Generously Leading the Optimistic Way

Give me a 2 -3 lined quote that is original that encouraged the reader to own their glow.

"The way that you love you, sets the tone how others will love you." "You do not have to be amazing at everything. Find your lane and roll therein!" – Zakiya M. Knighten

G.L.O.W. for me means seeing myself from God's Love Lenses, Outlook, and His Witness. Tell me, with this definition in mind, when you came to see yourself from this view and what this meant for your life up to this point. How has it caused you to show up in life?

Seeing myself from this view causes me to show up as a leader to follow THE LEADER! I understand my position, but I still show up to listen. I understand my part to play, but I fully understand that God pays for what He orders. So, when it comes to outlook, witness, or even seeing myself as He sees me, I will be victorious, as long as I am obedient and remain connected to the VINE!

www.killerconnections.com

www.befierceuniversity.com

www.relationshiprecode.com

Social Media:

FB: zakiyamonique

IG: zakiyamoniquespeaks

YT: RelationshipTV with Zakiya Monique

Book: *Killer Connections*

We Glowing! GlowVersation with
Pastor/Prophetess Eboni Gordon

When you think of the word "glow" what do you think of first? Paint me a picture...

When I think about glow. I think about the movie the last dragon when ShoNuff was drowning the young man and when he got up, he had this bright glow that gave him power. That was the 1st time that I remember saying like wow I want power like that that gives me a glow. I want to shine so bright that whatever tries to drown me it will be taken back by the glow that is endowed with power.

Now, when you think of a God-given GLOW, what is the first thing that comes to mind?

beauty, radiance, power, transformation. I think about having him in my life and being a beacon of light! I think about how he shows up before me and allows people to come into an awareness that there was darkness.

What did life look like for you before your glow presented itself?

It was dark, I was a mess, and did not like looking at myself. I didn't want anyone else to look at me either. I was broken, abandoned, rejected, alone, frustrated, forsaken, taken for granted.

Give me your own acronym for G.L.O.W.

God's Love Outweighs the Weight!

Give me a 2 -3 lined quote that is original that encouraged the reader to own their glow.

"Girl glow and show that you got what it takes! Your fun, loving heart says let's celebrate! Go Shine that light from in your soul and don't let it go. Let your soul glow!!" – Prophetess Eboni Gordon

G.L.O.W. for me means seeing myself from God's Love Lenses, Outlook, and His Witness. Tell me, with this definition in mind, when you came to see yourself from this view and what this meant for your life up to this point. How has it caused you to show up in life?

I remember hearing a song from my mom as a little girl she used to sing "Amazing Grace shall always be my song of praise, He looked beyond all my faults and saw my needs." The fact that he knew I would go through so much I believe His love covered me and saw me through his telescopic view before I even was a thought s and was sure that when he came in to my life I would be a great witness to all that entails. I am determined to let my glow shine bright because I know He looked beyond my faults and saw my needs.

www.theswopnetwork.com

Social Media:

FB, IG: swopnetwork

We Glowing! Glow Versation with
Bishop Landa Washington

When you think of the word "glow" what do you think of first? Paint me a picture...

When I think of glow, it means brightness, freshness, purity, joy, seeing the warm sunshine, feeling the warmth on my skin.

Now, when you think of a God-given GLOW, what is the first thing that comes to mind?

The warm touch of God. Knowing He is with me. The soft touch of comfort and strength.

What did life look like for you before your glow presented itself?

Sad, dull, meaningless, no purpose. The question of WHY.

Give me your own acronym for G.L.O.W

G= God's L=Love O=Over the W=World

Give me a 2 -3 lined quote that is original that encouraged the reader to own their glow.

"Don't Loose Heart. Your Assignment is tied to Your Purpose and Your Purpose is tied To God's Plan for your life. Rise to your Purpose." – Bishop Landa Washington

G.L.O.W. for me means seeing myself from God's Love Lenses, Outlook, and His Witness. Tell me, with this definition in mind, when you came to see yourself from this view and what this meant for your life up to this point. How has it caused you to show up in life?

Knowing God has a plan and purpose for my life, give me meaning. It helps me with the "WHY". To be honest most want to know the "why" and as I journey in this life and see myself from God's view - point I now see and understand the why factor.

My brothers and sisters I have encountered on this journey, I now know why. Throughout life's tribulations I have learned that coming together is the beginning, keeping together is a process and working together in the Word of God is true success. It is the focus of my ministry which seeks to connect sons, daughters, sisters, brothers, mothers, fathers, husbands, and wives with God.

My journey of pain, heartbreak, disappointment, loneliness, troubles, failures, etc were all because God's WHY for me and knowing that I can face tomorrow with the GLOW.

www.7Holistic.Com

Followersoftheway52@gmail.com

Stcyrw2@gmail.com

Social Media:

FB: Bishop Landa Washington

Power Word Power Thoughts of The Day Facebook Live

Books: Does This Gift Comes With Instructions: Parenting God's Way

Ten Keys To The First Lady

The Power Of A People That Pray

How To Maintain Your Joy.

Find them all on Amazon

Your
Personal
G.L.O.W.
Journal

Assignment 1 -

_____
_____
_____
_____
_____
_____
_____
_____
_____
_____
_____
_____
_____
_____
_____
_____
_____
_____
_____
_____
_____
_____
_____
_____
_____
_____
_____
_____

Assignment 2 -

_____
_____
_____
_____
_____
_____
_____
_____
_____
_____
_____
_____
_____
_____
_____
_____
_____
_____
_____
_____
_____
_____
_____
_____
_____
_____
_____
_____

Assignment 3 -

_____
_____
_____
_____
_____
_____
_____
_____
_____
_____
_____
_____
_____
_____
_____
_____
_____
_____
_____
_____
_____
_____
_____
_____
_____
_____
_____
_____

Assignment 4 -

_____
_____
_____
_____
_____
_____
_____
_____
_____
_____
_____
_____
_____
_____
_____
_____
_____
_____
_____
_____
_____
_____
_____
_____
_____
_____
_____
_____
_____

You Glowing -

_____
_____
_____
_____
_____
_____
_____
_____
_____
_____
_____
_____
_____
_____
_____
_____
_____
_____
_____
_____
_____
_____
_____
_____
_____
_____
_____
_____
_____

You Glowing -

You Glowing -

You Glowing -

You Glowing -

You Glowing -

You Glowing -

You Glowing -

If You Don't Own This Work Be Sure You Order Your Copy Today! Look Out For All Things That Are
Shalonda "Treasure" Williams a.k.a.
The Nspirational Treasure
www.TheInspirationalTreasure.com

- The Certified Life Coach
- The Inspirational/Transformational Speaker
- The Apostolic Prophet/Pastor

Follow On Social Media:
FB, IG, YouTube
@NspirationalTreasure